FED-UP

WITH FITNESS?

FED-UP WITH FITNESS?
Copyright © 2022 by Pamela Aye Simon MS, RD, LDN

Published in the United States of America
ISBN   Paperback: 978-1-959165-32-3
ISBN   eBook: 978-1-959165-33-0

All rights reserved. No part of this publication may be reproduced, stored in a retrieval system or transmitted in any way by any means, electronic, mechanical, photocopy, recording or otherwise without the prior permission of the author except as provided by USA copyright law.

The opinions expressed by the author are not necessarily those of ReadersMagnet, LLC.

ReadersMagnet, LLC
10620 Treena Street, Suite 230 | San Diego, California, 92131 USA
1.619. 354. 2643 | www.readersmagnet.com

Book design copyright © 2022 by ReadersMagnet, LLC. All rights reserved.

Cover design by Ericka Obando
Interior design by Daniel Lopez

FED-UP

WITH FITNESS?

Ditch the Clubs, Classes,
Guilt and Shame...

Pamela Aye Simon MS, RD, LDN

Table of Contents

DEDICATION vii

INTRODUCTION ix

MISSION xi

FUNNY FITNESS ACTIVITIES xv

Warning 31

Epilogue 63

About the Author 64

DEDICATION

To My Mom

And

For My Daughter

INTRODUCTION

Are you sick and tired of feeling guilty
for not being/staying in shape?
Have you had it with fitness advice and
failed exercise plans or classes?
Let's admit it …
It's difficult to squeeze out time in a day
for exercise.
Motivation can be even harder than time to find,
at least for me.
So I've come up with really clever exercises,
some you can fit into your schedule…
because they are part of your schedule.
Some are just fun.
Confused? Me too.
But, read on, my friend.
You won't regret it!

MISSION

The purpose of this book is to shine a light of humor on the
frustrations a person can experience in the fitness process.
As a health care professional and dietitian,
I try to guide clients towards
healthy weight and fitness goals;
but the fitness world has become
so instructive and judgmental.
It seems that the more seriously we
pursue our goals,
the fatter we get!
The quest for fitness has
lost its sense of humor.
Let's lighten up!
Let's move with joy!

Let's create individualized fitness plans
which give comfort
and make us laugh.
Maybe then we will want to do this!

Pam

Please Remember:

The exercises in this book are not intended
to be taken seriously.
Their safety levels haven't been tested.
(Translation: Don't blame me if you get hurt!)

However...

The activities in this book are intended

to add laughter to your fitness efforts,

and to encourage you to add your own

fitness movements to routine tasks.

Fitness is movement...

So move, twist, and stretch

any body part you can...anywhere you can...

And you will find your own fitness.

FUNNY FITNESS ACTIVITIES

SHOE AEROBICS

Always, buy shoes that are too big for you.

These shoes are hard to keep on your feet -

especially if you are in a hurry.

The gyrations and foot muscle movements

you have to go through to keep them on

are great lower leg and foot exercises.

If you lose a shoe,

and it flies off your foot,

it might hurt someone.

More importantly -

you would look really stupid.

MALL ACTIVITY

Walk backwards really fast around the mall.

You can try to avoid colliding with other people,

but running into people burns more calories.

Just sayin'...

BOWLING FUN

Instead of regular bowling,

try a game by knocking down pins

with your feet.

All of that alley walking is

good cardiovascular exercise.

Plus, kicking the pins down

helps with anger management.

ISOTONIC DRIVING

Drive your car with the seat

tilted really far back

That way, you have to do sit-ups

every time you reach for the steering wheel.

SKIPPING SNACKS

Make yourself skip every time you

get a snack from the kitchen.

And don't hang-out in the kitchen

just to avoid a skip trip.

I mean it...

Oh...and try to choose only snacks

that won't spill as you skip...

unless you want to add rug cleaning

to your exercise routine.

I mean it's not much fun,

but it does burn calories...

SIDE-SWIPES

Find a running trail or path.

Run side-ways as fast as you can.

You will need a rear-view mirror

on your head

so you don't run into people

or fall off a cliff.

Try not to break the mirror, though.

You know what that means...

FREE FOOD WEIGHTS

For strength training, bring all of the food

from your snack cabinet or fridge

into your hang-out room,

one item at a time.

This is what I call "free (food) weights."

After you are done snacking,

take each item, one at a time,

back to its storage place.

This is what I call

"Clean up your mess."

SEEING STAIRS

———∞∞∞———

Always go up and down

stairs, steps, or ramps

on your tip-toes.

Your calf muscles will thank you!

Or - if your toes don't work too well,

walk in a circle on each step.

Hold onto the railing, though.

You can't exercise from a hospital bed.

CARDIO TEETH

Run in place while you brush your teeth.

This will give you 2 minutes

of cardio exercise

each time you brush.

Plus, the bumpier your running stride is,

the more stimulation your gums get!

WARNING: If your gums start bleeding,

you are too clumsy for this exercise...

(or ANY exercise, really).

BEDTIME CRAWL

Every bedtime,

crawl from the bedroom door

to your bed, and then

crawl up onto your bed.

Crawling uses muscles you don't use much,

(and may never need).

This is in the exercise category called

"just in case,"

for the rarely used muscle groups.

(Skip this exercise if you really don't care.)

FACERSIZE

Your face needs exercise too, so …

… every time you drive alone,

make faces.

Make all kinds of faces -

scary faces, happy faces, worried faces, etc.

Re-e-e-ally use those face muscles!

Careful though…

Don't distract other drivers too much,

or you just be making faces at the police.

WAIST MANAGEMENT

When you sit down to work on your

laptop, desktop or tablet,

place the computer behind you.

This way, you will have to twist at the waist

to navigate the screen or

type on the keyboard.

It may be more difficult to work this way

and your messages may look like nonsense,

but you will have a thinner waist in no time.

What could be more important than that?

FALLING FOR HEALTH

In the previous exercise,

falling off your chair periodically

is a good thing.

Struggling back up onto the chair

is great for lower body and arm strength.

P.S.
If you can't get back up,

delete this exercise from your routine...

SHOP IT OFF

When you go shopping,

instead of just walking down the aisles

with the products you want to buy,

walk up and down every aisle really fast.

Only slow down to pick up your needed items.

By the time you're ready to check out,

You've added cardio-exercises to your day!

DOG WALK - IN REVERSE

Instead of walking your dog,

let the dog walk you.

Actually, if you let the dog lead you,

I think you will be running -

all around yards, trees, gutters, rocks, etc.

Be prepared to stop and start suddenly.

What a great work-out!

FYI - This activity is in the category of

exercise that fitness-land people call

"extreme."

DAY AFTER DOG-WALK

Run around to all your neighbors

who saw you

behaving strangely yesterday,

and who may have yard damage

from your activity,

and apologize and explain.

(Good luck with that...)

CAT WALK

Yes, this is even better cardio exercise.

Take your cat for a walk.

Go everywhere your cat goes.

EVERYWHERE.

The only problem with this activity is that

you may end up stuck in a tree.

So be prepared.

LAWN-CARDIO

When you mow your grass,

try using a manual push mower

instead of that powered one.

For the best work-out,

Mow the whole lawn on your tip-toes.

You will burn so many calories,

you can eat anything you want that day.

WARNING:

This is a high risk activity (I think).

BEACH TIME

Go to a beach with lots of sandy area

leading to the water.

Do somersaults all the way

to the water's edge.

You may get dizzy, and really sore.

But think of the exercise potential!

FYI:

This last activity was the idea

of a 5-year-old,

so maybe just walking to the water's edge

is better for safety at your age.

You decide...

FLOOR FITNESS

If you own a pet hamster, a pet rat,

a gerbil, or other pet rodent,

get on the floor next to the cage

and open the cage door.

Once the furry creature runs

out of the cage, give it

a 2 to 3-minute head-start.

Crawl really fast after your pet to

catch and cage it again.

Presto! Cardio for you AND your rodent!

P.S. You may need knee pads for this one.

REVERSE CHAIR YOGA

Chair yoga is a wonderful

strength-training activity,

a great option if you are tired or sore.

But it can get boring.

So...for a fun challenge,

sit in your chair backwards!

I haven't tried this yet,

but it sounds fun,

doesn't it?

No?

MIND OVER MIRROR

---⊷∞⊶---

If you like to work-out in front of a mirror,

I have a better idea.

Get 2 Fun-House mirrors,

(like from a Circus).

One mirror should be the one that makes

you look really wide or fat.

The second mirror should make you

look real tall and thin.

Hang the first mirror and do your usual

exercise routine in front of it everyday.

After a few weeks, replace the fat mirror

with the thin mirror.

Exercise in front of it for a few weeks.

Can you feel it?

I mean, you probably didn't get slimmer

or grow taller.

But you FEEL like you did.

Who cares about reality?

KITCHEN KICK LINE

Doing dishes can be great cardio fun!

Here's how: With each dish you wash

or load into the dishwasher,

do a backward or forward leg kick.

Just be careful that you don't accidentally

kick your pet dog in the process

On the down side,

my poor dog hates the kitchen now,

(She isn't too crazy about me either.)

On the up side,

my kick form and leg muscles

are in great shape!

Plus, my family and friends

Are afraid of me now...

(Is this a good or bad thing?)

JUMP & REACH

Arrange your kitchen so that all of your

frequently used items are stored on the

highest shelves or tallest cupboards.

That way, you have to jump, reach or climb

frequently to fix and eat food you love.

Brilliant, right?

No cheating, though.

Using a ladder, a stool or

a tall friend wouldn't be fair...

Oh...and if YOU are really tall.

you are automatically disqualified,

(and you have to give me your food).

WRIST ACTION

Your wrists need exercise too.

But how? Easy!

When you are someplace in hot weather,

instead of turning on the air conditioning,

use your wrist action to fan yourself

with your hands!

This is what I call a "win/win" activity.

Not only have you created coolness,

you have stronger wrists!

Warning:

Just don't slap yourself in the face

by accident with your fanning hands.

And don't try this while driving.

MOVE IT

If you really need daily exercise and you want to help people at the same time, take a drive in the morning looking for moving trucks or U-Hauls.

Offer to help anyone who seems to be moving.

This is better than weight-lifting, right?

Just don't leer at people.

You might end up in jail...

SHOE CHEW

If you don't have one, buy or borrow a puppy.

Before you go to bed, place all of your shoes

in a location the puppy has access to.

Go to sleep.

The next morning,

try to find a matching pair of shoes

which are not obviously chewed up.

Search everywhere.

Look up, down, and under.

You may even have to crawl on the floor

to get the puppy's prospective.

By the time you find matching shoes,

you will have completed your

morning exercise routine!

Pamela Aye Simon MS, RD, LDN

Can't find a matching pair?

P.S. Walgreens has rubber sandals
for $9.99
(just in case you need to get
matching shoes on the way to work).

DOG HOP

If you own more than one dog, and maybe a

cat or two, simple activities like

walking around your home

can be an agility challenge.

Just coming in the front door can be chaos!

To avoid tripping over or stepping on

a dog or cat, you have to

hop, slide, jump over,

and sometimes stop suddenly.

This Dog Hop challenge provides a much

better work-out if your dogs aren't trained

to follow commands or, even better,

if they don't listen to you at all.

(I should know...)

Pamela Aye Simon MS, RD, LDN

TONGUE FUN

Did you ever notice that your tongue muscles get weaker as you age? I mean it gets harder to lick Oreo crumbs off of your lips (you end up wearing them all day and no one tells you), right? It's also more of a challenge to retrieve ice cream drips running from your mouth.

WHY?
Because your tongue muscles need exercise!

Try this activity for

―⊗⊗⊗―

increasing tongue fitness:

Move your tongue every which way...

up, down, out, in, sideways, and around.

It is OK to look ugly in this exercise.

It feels good and helps flexibility.

Warning:

Just don't do this activity around little kids.

They will take it personally and you know what that means...

EASY RAFT FLOAT

If you love lying on a blow-up raft

in a pool, lake, river, etc.,

but you have trouble getting

on the raft in the water,

try this brilliant idea:

Tie the raft to your backside

with a rope around your waist.

(FYI: Walking to the water with the raft

attached is really good cardio exercise.)

Now...walk into the water about 2 feet

and just fall backwards...

Presto!

You are floating on the raft

without falling or tripping into the water!

Enjoy!

But just so you know, I have no idea how to

get out of the water with the raft attached

without creating a scene or calling 911.

Maybe you could bring your own rescue team?

TV CARDIO

When watching TV, put your comfy chair on the opposite side of the room from the TV screen. Whenever you want to change channels or adjust controls, run to the TV and back. Take the remote with you because a lot of TV's don't have control buttons anymore. So for this activity, you have to pretend...

MARCH FOR YOUR HEART

If you are a person who likes to attend football games and/or parades, this activity is perfect for your cardio health. Whenever you attend an event that has a marching band performance, get ready to participate! As they march by, just join in the routine. March right along with the band. Not only will you get your exercise for the day, you will be part of the show!

If you are a person

who looks like a real dork

when you march or dance,

(you know who you are)

please do not do this activity...

...Please.

ESCALATE FOR EXERCISE

You will need an escalator for this activity,

The exercise is simple.

Just go up the down escalator and

down the up escalator...

as fast as you can and

as many times as you can.

If the venue and escalators are busy,

make sure people can see you coming

by using a bright reflective vest and/or a

bike light on your head.

A disguise might be a good idea too.

You don't want anyone to recognize you

As you do this idiotic behavior...do you?

(unless you already have this reputation).

DRAG WALKING

―⦅⦆―

To increase the exercise intensity of your

daily walks, find, borrow, or buy

a stroller, wagon, or shopping cart.

Fill it with something heavy (rocks, bricks,

dirty laundry, or junk from your garage).

Push or pull the wheeled item

anytime you go on a walk.

I mean, sure, your walk won't be as pleasant.
(It might even be a little painful.)
And your neighbors might
question your sanity.
But...

Think of the benefits!!

You get great cardio training.

Plus, you might get rid of

some of that junk

in

your

garage!

BIKE CHALLENGE

If you are a bicycle kind of person,

for your next bicycle ride,

take the seat off.

Now your legs get an intense work-out!

Just don't forget you took the seat off...

Trying to sit down while riding

without a seat

could get really ugly.

(I mean, *I* wouldn't want to see it...
and I work in Healthcare.)

SPACE

Once a week, rearrange the furniture and other items in your living space to a different configuration.

This activity is great for strength-training.

If you do it really fast,

it's a good cardio workout too.

Plus...try this...

Each time you rearrange your stuff,

test your memory.

Turn off all the lights

And count the number of times you

stub a toe,

crash into something,

slip and fall,

or knock something over.

(You could keep score,
but nobody will care...)

PING PONG UNLIMITED

―――⌇⌇⌇―――

But first, a story...

When I was 14 years old, my dad bought the family a ping pong table and net, balls, etc.
He put it in an empty room in the basement.
Although we didn't really know much about ping pong, my mom and I decided to break the new equipment in.
I mean, how hard could it be?
Well, after the first 5 minutes, it was obvious that the little net on the table
just slowed things down.
We decided to just take the net off.
Much easier that way.
Within the next 5 minutes, we realized that the game was more fun if we didn't worry about keeping the little ball on the table.
Better yet!

Mom and I were now playing a wild form of racket ball with
paddles and really bouncy balls.
No area was out of bounds,
The aim of the game
was to just keep the ball bouncing...
off the floor, the ceiling, the walls.
Hitting the ball became more difficult
as our fits of laughter increased.

Nobody won. Nobody lost.

But Mom and I were so worn out...

from the exercise
AND
the laughter!

This is fitness activity at its best.

WARNINGS FROM A FITNESS FAILURE EXPERT

Don't Run Your Toes Off

If you are an avid jogger or runner,

you need to be warned.

After years of pounding

your feet on surfaces,

your toe joints may disintegrate!

I am OK now.

(I mean, after 2 surgeries

and nails placed to rebuild joints.)

But the experts told me

to never run again.

(What a relief!!)

Flip Flop Running

OK...

I know that most of you know

to exercise in appropriate shoes.

It's not rocket science, right?

Well, for a person who started running

at age 10, and in the late 1960's,

I did not know that going for a quick run

in flip flops was idiotic behavior.

My warning to you is this:
If you run in flip flops
you risk scraping off
the top of your big toe.
And it hurts!
Enough said.

Dollar Socks

I love the Dollar Store.

But I just have a little warning

about Dollar Store socks:

If you wear this store's sock product
for exercises, activities, or anything
except lying down or sitting in one place,
your feet will become the color of the socks.
It doesn't come off easily either.
Also, if you think you are safer
with white socks...
the endless white fuzz
deposited between your toes
makes up for the lack of color transfer.
...Just sayin'...

Gymnasts' Necks

I noticed at the Olympics this year

that most of the gymnasts had necks

almost as wide as their heads

(kind of like my French Bulldog).

My warning to you is this:

If you are interested in or involved in
the sport of gymnastics,
you might develop a big neck.

(Good to know, right?)

Archie Comics Role Model

When I was a preteen,

my body shape role model was

Betty from the Archie Comics Books.

Bad idea...

My warning to you:

Choose a normally-shaped human being
to be the body-shape you admire.
Better yet, love yourself as you are.
You don't need to change your body
to be acceptable or adorable.
You are that now.

Don't Pole Vault in the Woods

(This one I learned from my brother)

I will just start this warning
with the warning:

Don't offer to catch the pole
of a pole vaulter
who has built his
pit in the woods.

I don't have the energy to explain.
But if you need the warning, you will know.
For the rest of you, just let it go.

Motivation Killer

They make it look so good in the ads.

Described as a "Complete Gym Set,"

it looks wonderful!

It comes with weights, a pulley system,

and a bench for all kinds of

strength training activities.

What could be better?

So you order it online and...

The "Gym" is delivered to your home!

How easy is this?

Then you see what you ordered.
The enticing product comes
in about 10 boxes and 1000 pieces.
Plus, the directions for assembly
are either savagely complicated
or a bad joke.
You try to put it together...
But after four hours of effort,
with no structure appearing,
and pieces everywhere,
you are so frustrated and mad,
you can't take it anymore.
You never want to workout again!

So my warning is this:
Maybe this product has challenges
that could crush your fitness motivation.
So maybe...uh...don't order a total gym?
On the other hand,
what a great way to practice
anger management

Jelly Bean Toxicity

Jelly Bellies are wonderful!

Plus, these little taste delights

only have 2 calories each!

The problem is that

they are ADDICTIVE, right?

My warning is this:
Stop eating Jelly Bellies at 1000.
After eating 1000 pieces,
I have no idea what your body will do.
As for me, I get a sick feeling at 500 pieces.
And good luck out there...

Pain is Gain, Right?

How idiotic is that motto?

I mean, it's not even logical!

My warning is this:
Pain is NOT gain.
Pain is insane!
It is a bad thing.
If you have real pain while you move.
you need to go to the doctor.

However, a little muscle soreness
can be a good thing.
Not only does it mean you made progress,
it is a great excuse to get a massage
and *relax in a jacuzzi.*

Epilogue

Be you.

Fitness needs to FIT YOU.

Move because it feels good...

and free...

and empowering.

You are beautiful as you are.

And - Please - Above All Else-

BE HERE NOW

About the Author

Pamela Simon is a Master's level Registered Dietitian. She wrote "Fed-Up With Fitness?" to help readers laugh about their fitness challenges. In spite of her profession, Pam loves Twinkees and hates exercise classes.

"Movement should be natural and fun." In addition, she believes people need to enjoy eating again without thinking so hard. In Pam's words, "no one deserves to feel guilt for eating favorite foods or for not exercising."

"Life is much bigger than this!"

www.ingramcontent.com/pod-product-compliance
Lightning Source LLC
LaVergne TN
LVHW020431080526
838202LV00055B/5135